# Mom, Dad, who are The Beatles?
## THE BEATLES BIOGRAPHY FOR KIDS

Written and Illustrated
by Phyllis Matthew

PARADOXOLOGEÕ, CARMEL VALLEY, CA 93924

Mom, Dad, who are The Beatles? The Beatles Biography for Kids
Copyright © 2017 by Phyllis Mazzocchi
All rights reserved.
No part of this publication may be reproduced, distributed or transmitted in any form or by any means, including photocopying, recording or other electronic or mechanical methods, or by any information storage or retrieval system, without written permission from the publisher, except in the case of brief quotations embodied in a book review.
Printed in the United States of America.
For information, address:
Paradoxologeõ, P O Box 1803, Carmel Valley, CA 93924.
www.paradoxologeo.com

ISBN: 0-9861189-2-3
ISBN-13: 978-0-9861189-2-0
Library of Congress Control Number: 2017915162
Paradoxologeõ, Carmel Valley, CA

FOR FANS AND FUTURE FANS EVERYWHERE

Once there was a

very, very famous

Rock n' Roll band named

**THE BEATLES**

In fact, The Beatles were

**THE MOST FAMOUS**

Rock n' Roll band ever!

They looked different than anyone else,

They sounded different than anyone else,

and they played BEAUTIFUL MUSIC

that changed the face of the world.

World BEFORE Beatles	World AFTER Beatles

The members of THE BEATLES were four young lads from Liverpool, England, named

JOHN

PAUL

GEORGE

and RINGO

They had English accents and said funny words like Luv instead of Love and fab instead of fabulous.

They had long floppy haircuts
that went into their eyes,
and over their ears,
and down past their necks.

Before The Beatles came along,
people had much shorter hair

like this...　　　　　　or like this...

THE BEATLES wore funny looking suits with no collars and big boots with high heels. In fact, John, Paul, George and Ringo wore just about anything they pleased!

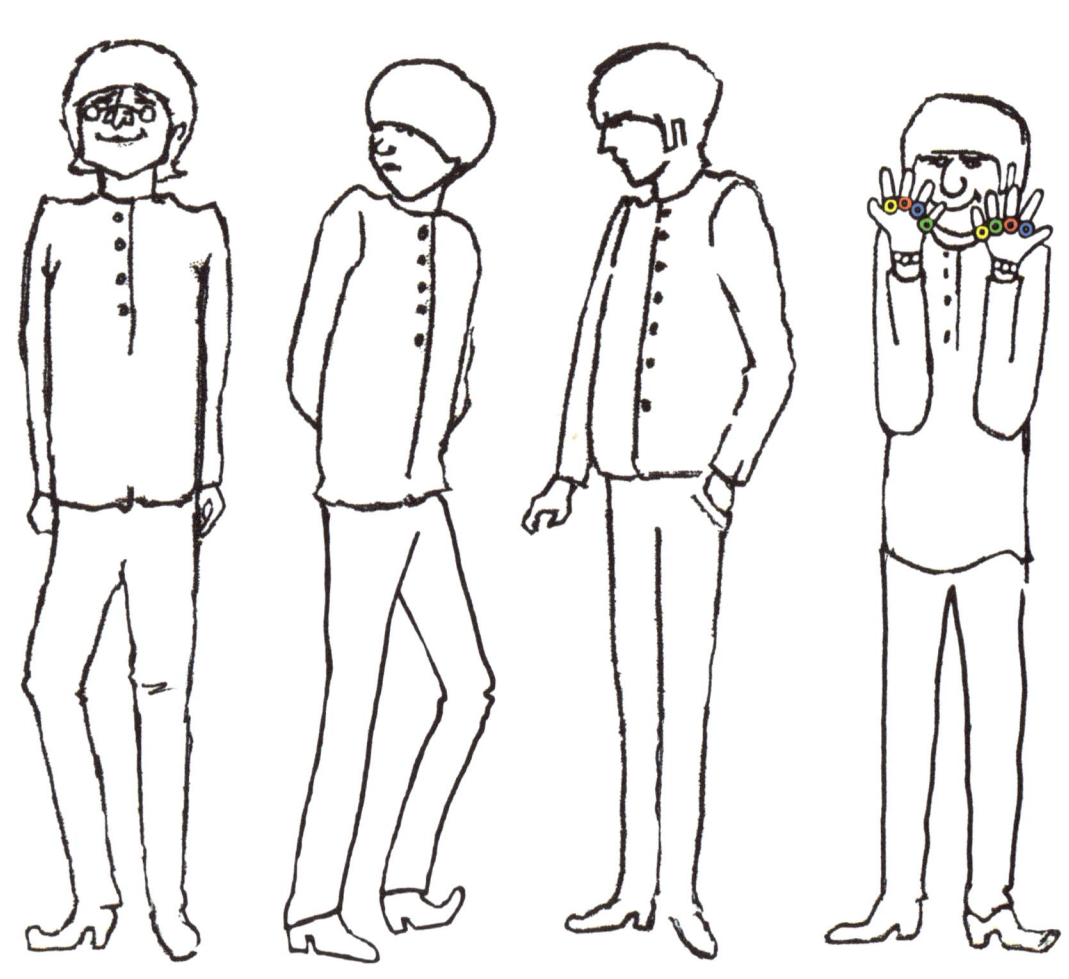

It was during this time that young people the world over also let their hair grow long, and they too, felt free to dress in all sorts of new ways. It was a time of change for EVERYONE.

But the most special thing
about The Beatles was their music!
The songs they sang had a certain sound that was different than anyone had ever heard before. The Beatles had what was called:

Charisma is a special feeling that makes you feel really good inside and out. And that's just what Beatle music could do - make you feel good ALL OVER.

ALL I'VE GOT TO DO

THANK YOU GIRL

HOLD ME TIGHT

I CALL YOUR NAME

TELL ME WHY

YOU CAN'T DO THAT

IF I FELL

ANY TIME AT ALL

WHEN I GET HOME

and many, many more...

People of ALL AGES enjoyed The Beatles' music, and before you knew it, Beatle songs were being played EVERYWHERE...

from THE FAR EAST

to THE BRiTiSH ISLES

# to AUSTRALIA

# to SOUTH AMERICA

# to the U S A

Everyone sang BEATLE songs and to this day, there are still some people who can sing EVERY word to EVERY song.

BEATLE fans loved John, Paul, George and Ringo **SO MUCH** that they could hardly hold it in. When The Beatles appeared on TV or at concerts, the fans would scream and squeal with delight.

They followed The Beatles everywhere, even to hotels and airports, just to catch a glimpse of their **FAVORITE BEATLE.**

Before you knew it, there were BEATLE dolls and BEATLE books, and BEATLE buttons and BEATLE clothes and even BEATLE wigs!

All of this excitement was called

## BEATLEMANIA

and excited Beatle fans were called

## BEATLEMANIACS

Each of The Beatles had a special personality and fans felt as if they knew them very well.

**JOHN** was the first member of the band.

He played Rhythm Guitar, harmonica, and sang lead vocals.

JOHN was witty, intelligent, and out-spoken.

He sang and wrote songs about peace, love and harmony for a better world.

JOHN reminded us that our Dreams are REAL and that our Dreams can come TRUE.

PAUL played Bass Guitar and sang lead vocals with John.

PAUL was known as the "romantic" Beatle for singing sweet love songs that made all the girls swoon.

Together, John and Paul wrote **the words and music** to most of The Beatle songs that are so popular today.

**GEORGE** was the Lead Guitarist of the group and sang background vocals.

**GEORGE** came to be known as the tall, dark-haired mysterious Beatle because of his cool, casual manner and his interest in the mystical teachings of India.

 RINGO played Drums in the band.

He was nicknamed RINGO for the many rings he wore, sometimes even two on each finger!

RINGO's zany antics and practical jokes made everybody smile.

JOHN, PAUL, GEORGE, and RINGO

continued to write and play songs together for many years to come.

They sang of imaginary people like

ELEANOR RIGBY & SARGEANT PEPPER

and faraway places like

PENNY LANE

and

STRAWBERRY FIELDS

The Beatles were always changing and always growing. And as fans listened to their music, they were changing and growing too!

THE BEATLES HELPED US LEARN THAT

**THERE'S NOTHING WE CAN'T DO!**

and

**ALL YOU NEED IS LOVE**

and much, much more!

TODAY, you can hear Beatle music just about anywhere...
on the radio and TV,
on your computer,
in the movie theatre,
in elevators,
and even in the Dentist's Office!

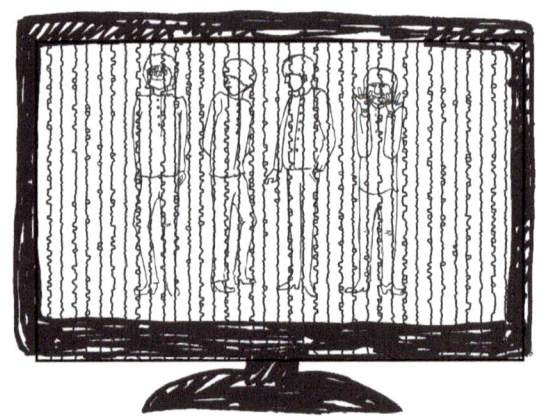

Young people who grew up in
THE SIXTIES will never forget
John, Paul, George and Ringo.

YEAH, YEAH, YEAH !
YEAH, YEAH, YEAH !

What were the names of the four Beatles?

Which Beatle liked to wear rings on every finger?

How many Beatle songs can you name?

How many Beatle songs can you sing?

How long will The Beatles' music live?
 a) a gazillion years
 b) a million billion trillion years
 c) FOREVER

www.ingramcontent.com/pod-product-compliance
Lightning Source LLC
Chambersburg PA
CBHW041119300426
44112CB00002B/31